Winter Verses

Also by Elmo Howell:
MISSISSIPPI HOME-PLACES:
Notes on Literature and History, 1988.

Elmo Howell

Winter Verses

Copyright © 1989 by Elmo Howell
All rights reserved.
For information, address:
E. H. Howell,
3733 Douglass Avenue,
Memphis, Tennessee 38111.

For
Hallie Howell Dyer

Contents

I. The Old Man

The Old Man	13
Old Acquaintance	15
Exodus	17
The Tombstone	19
The Lepers	21
Forty-Niner	23
The Dove	25
February	27
The Violet	29
Brother Pain	31

II. Neighbor Frog

The Brook	35
Neighbor Frog	37
Willows	39
The Burden	41
Sunup	43
The Arrowhead	45
The New Whippoorwill	47
The Dogwood Tree	49
The Midge	51
Spring Morning	53

III. Heart's-Ease

The Unfinished Bird's-Nest	57
The White Butterfly	59
Heart's-Ease	61
The Eunuch	63
The Opera	65
The Robbers	67
The Trip	69
Love Song	71
The Robin	73

IV. The Home-Place

Stopping By	77
The Home-Place	79
Decoration Day	81
Leaving	83
The Note	85
The Whippoorwills	87
The Wanton	89
The Bluebird	91
The Cornfield	93

V. Fall Morning

Fall Morning	97
Goldenrod	99
Fido	101
The Snake	103
Cedars	105
Historical Marker	107
Putting My Dog to Sleep	109
The Little Moth	111
The Fugitives	113
The Blessing	115

VI. Nightshade

The Virgin	119
In the Radiation Therapy Waiting Room	121
The Beacon	123
Old Maids	125
The Daisy Tree	127
Vieux Carré	129
Assumption	131
Nightshade	133

VII. Bright Star!

The Cedar	137
Bright Star!	139
The Rabbit	141
Ponderosas	143
Layover	145
The Swallow	147
The Elect	149
Cattle	151
Sparrows	153

I.
The Old Man

The Old Man

In January the mockingbird,
Who knocks about the sky in May,
Sprints in a naked bush close to the ground.
When I pass by, he pops out as if to tell
    me something
But never says a word;
And sometimes waits (Is it only for an
    apple core?)
On a wire by my window.
A gentleman chorister on leave!
But his silence is not like that of other
    birds.
How could it be
After the white nights
With two o'clock floating to the west from
    the light pole?
Can a fellow turn monk, denying song,
Not vying with stars!
Or is he only an old man now---
Come down to that, trying to tell me!---
Settling for a low tight bush
And good quiet neighbors?

Old Acquaintance

I felt no dash or hurt when I heard;
    Death's incivilities are not new---
    All to set right in a day or two---
But day draws in in a word.

Yesterday he came and gave me his hand,
    And sat awhile and talked of the rain
    And other dear encumbrances that remain
When old men shuffle them back to bone.

Exodus

By order assembled here,
    A lean diminished band,
We hug our idols in the dark
    And wait the last command:

Time's reft pensioners
    Cast on Sinai's track
Counting dead shekels
    In the long look back.

No more the silver dishes,
    The graved goblets of gold;
Gone the braids and tresses
    And ivory to hold.

O fleshpots of Egypt!
    On this dusty plain
The cry of fullness in the night
    Not to come again.

The Tombstone

After the canebrake,
With burden precautionary
We came to the wooded headland,
Cedared in silence
And foulness like a homesite.
While the others looked for the spot---
Not really very sure but made a quick
    decision---
I leant on brown rails arched,
By lettered flowers
Valorously rising out of the beetle's dust---
And chanced on revelation:
That the world did not begin with me,
Not even with the new graveyard by the church
Where the old are still looked after,
Still called on in the slack of Sunday
    afternoon.
What breath,
What rack of time blew on these hills?
Down what still corridors
Ever expanding
From the certain point of this June morning?
Do these bones belong to me,
Grandiloquent in chard and curlicue rust,
Smiling on dim votaries
("Whose children, these!")
Racing again towards the pickup?

The Lepers

Do the dead listen
    As mornings pass
For a stir of feet
    In the waiting grass
Before the full tide
    And urgent beat
Of manly pride
    About the street?

Do they have time
    In their work below
For one look back
    To the rising glow,
Or evening round
    Of whippoorwill
And the settling down
    Across the hill?

Or is it all done there,
    Love deferred,
No poor heart's fever
    Of hope or a bird?
Not even a glance
    At how the world knocks,
Cold and askance
    In a private box?

Forty-Niner

The garden is black.
Tomato vines crumple at the stake
With old rags naked that held them up,
And milk cartons in the ground where we
    watered them.
The sun settles dead on her tablecloth.
I keep on thinking she'll be back.

The Dove

I heard the dove on a January morning
In deep frost,
Somewhere against the eastern light.
Winter had settled down to banked fires and
    close measure
And joy surprised us.
Bobbing on the wide expanse, neat, unsinkable,
We feared deployment, the olive leaf plucked off.
But the bird came back---before we were ready---
Ardent at daylight,
With news about the gaudy tents
And rabble-crowded shore.

February

Month of uncertainties,
Brief in sun and ice.
Warm skies betray old men,
Unsettle the deal they made
    with themselves,
Disturb the rhythm of the peach.
Shag-end of days.
In-between month
Of panic sprout
And sick longing for January peace.

The Violet

I found a violet in a dell
Where winter woods had come to grief
Tending house, snug and well,
And watching the weather under a leaf;

Close from the wind and wildcat's foot,
Holding up its vassal due
From essence stored under a root
A strict economy of blue.

Brother Pain

Touch me, Brother Pain, in the night deep!
Arraign me in the dross of sleep.
For the day's fair alms my only good
To fall beneath thy rod.

Purge the dark and fashion new!
Set me on a morning blue---
Shut of rot and wound within,
Quick to fly again!

II.
Neighbor Frog

The Brook

The February sun, high above ice,
Sang in the gutter like a mountain brook;
While I, resentful of change,
Trudged happy in being winter-hearted.
Who wants the green again? Better to stare
    from a hole,
Keep to ice
Loosened only a little about the feet.
But the windless day gave notice!
And the new sun (When did it get this way?)
Disturbed the old lair.
The brook rang, out, Make way, Make way for joy!
And the foolish heart, with a skip and a beat,
Just for the fun of it---Can you imagine?---
Joined, dared!
What sail awaits this rustic tide---
And what fair wind?
What sea! What sea!

Neighbor Frog

On this bright morning
    Of leaf and sun,
What quitrent have I paid,
    What mercy done,
To merrily croak
    Like neighbor frog
Embracing heaven
    In a bog?

Drunk with light,
    Soused in luck
(A quiver reft
    Out of a rock),
With a dragonfly
    Upon the bud!
Blink an eye---
    Back to mud.

Willows

I think that willows are fey young girls
Dancing by the brookside in new dresses,
Ready for the party long before the others.
They beckon to join them, "Come, give all!"
Not seeing beyond April,
Petulant, in the rain weeping,
Showing their buds.

Willows come out before the year is ready,
Not really a tree at all,
But pretty young girls
Or a diffident boy, troubling, virginal,
Making a face at life.
Back in the woods, the old trees wait,
Frowning on charade.
Willows are playful, shaping through mist a
    wisp of new green,
Calling, calling.
But not trees. Not trees at all.

The Burden

A woods smoke in March
    Before the new green
When the boughs in the orchard
    Are silver and clean;
When the mule lifts his tail
    To the garden plough,
And the redbird stutters,
    Trying out joy---
Puts more on the heart
    In promises sweet
Than threescore black winters
    And ten of sleet.

Sunup

I don't dare go into my garden early in
 the morning!
So much extremity at the time of roses and
 honeysuckle
That once in the pull, no way back to shore.
I stand in the kitchen door and look out.
Is it the dew, or only the yellow sun striking
 broad,
Or trees caught up in the redolence of sleep?
I must wait here.
A robin sees me,
And, ah, I left my shears on the walk.
An hour or so and gold will pass---the clock
 will see to that.
These things must be managed and require a
 strong hand.

The Arrowhead

When the plow turned up a broken flint,
He sat on the ground to consider,
Among other things,
Means of propulsion in a land of no Sundays.
Out of the dark before Presidents,
A palpable shot from alder and birch
On calendar, probate court,
And a garden paling fence.
But who was he to face up to such matters
While a mule stomped and waited?
Spirits about the earth,
No doubt about that!
Lurking by the creekside
Or in deep shade by the waterbucket.
At dark they close in with whippoorwills,
Cajoling, threatening,
Poor landless souls, stalking a boy's dream;
Coming very close past midnight,
Teasing,
Even in the tree by the smokehouse.

The New Whippoorwill

Unheralded, the new whippoorwill,
    Intact of sudden North,
Lords the night on my April hill
    In claim of startled earth.

Where now is the old voice of spring,
    The tribal flux of joy and woe
In bright notes from a sky darkling?
    Where do the lost spirits go?

Before two mighty armies stood,
    Imperious, poles apart,
What beauty struck my piece of wood?
    What beak laid out the bloody chart?

The Dogwood Tree

In March, I found the dogwood tree---
A glistening white canopy
In leant oblation to the sun
For its sweet perfection.

Affirmation like a lark!
Then back again to burr and bark.
But in the breath of sacrament
Before the rush of beauty went

(Before all suns kick in to cold
And strategy of sense to mold),
It stood an hour against the night
And was immeasurably bright.

The Midge

When I consider big things and little things
And the accepted good fortune of some men;
When I think of leviathan shouldering the deep
And this midge thrown up in the bath of my eye,
Drying his wings on my finger
And edging again towards enterprise---
I ask myself,
"How big is joy?
What proof do you have---
When a light wind lifts on a summer day
And bids fair journey?"

Spring Morning

April is a gremlin month,
Disturbing winter's ritual grief
In witchery of new leaf.
Woods smoke drifts across the hill,
The new sun tries the will.
On a windy bank, too soon for rose,
Violet blows,
And the field lark knows.

In the newborn breath between
Misty reach of blue and green
Plummet bird and bee.
Barefoot children leap and laugh,
The old cow finds her calf,
And the pasture spring
With flush and flash of gauzy wing
Sets off for faery sea.

III.
Heart's-Ease

The Unfinished Bird's-Nest

Something happened in my hawthorn tree!
All April long blossom and bee
Coupled in sweet, but redbird dear
Quit the lists in mystery.

What wee illusion foundered there?
What beastie version of despair
Beside the last half-mortised leaf
In the blue house-building air?

The White Butterfly

Beauty marked the end of joy.
    The blue day leapt and sang,
But on the pierced and lifted brow
    The maimed years empty hung.
When out of the hermit's stony cell
    A white butterfly on laboring wing!
A spirit surely, to break the spell
And sign to craven flesh all's well---
    If the desert god allow such thing.

Heart's-Ease

After you left, I went into the garden,
    But the flowers had nothing to say,
Busy with the sun, and could only glisten
    In their prim array:
Roses tumbling as they were taught to do
    And, in a mix of old red
Guarded by spears of spiderwort blue,
    Sweet sweet William in a private bed.
As if a rainbow and all the spice
    Kindled by an April sun
Could stay the narrowing of ice,
    Or reach to what this day's done.
Beauty, how vain and careless to reckon
    With canker and the hateful doomed:
Only a shut door spoke or had the time to listen,
    And the gray worn steps where nothing bloomed.

The Eunuch

Where, where is sovereign joy?
In the appointed round of mirth
With flower, friend, book or love's toy?
    Is it at all on earth,

    Or in that far realm of light
Summoned in gold by a Sanctus bell,
For the better sort who pierce the night
    And report all's well?

    Or just in all fever spent?---
Biding poor fools in the round of brawn,
A eunuch napping by a silken tent
    Before the slop of dawn?

The Opera

On Saturday afternoon we listen to the opera,
Washing the car or hauling out the rug---
Or lying in bed against the rain or cold:
An hour or so from the week's commitment
For voices and the long stare.
Flesh is sad against the swell of horns
And usualness of three o'clock,
Dragged round to be looked at.
But keeps a stiff upper lip,
Preens a little, picks at plumage over the shoulder,
With Lucia screaming down the years, mad, mad,
Trailing love.

The Robbers

When the robbers came and took my gold,
Bustling about from wall to wall
Like thoughtless children in their play,
They did no mischief bold---
The chairs are long set right,
The splintered boxes swept away---
But left a stain upon my lintel bright
To clutch and hold
When I come home at night,
Feeding on the rarities of day,
And won't go away.

The Trip

After it was over, which could never be over,
We went away.
It seemed the right thing to do.
And the dry white light of the plains,
The sudden escarpment and mesquite-covered hills
(Which never seemed to violate the flatness)
And pistol sun at day's end
Were just what we wanted.
Sitting with a drink in the blank hotel,
Right-angled to a sandbed---
Matron to a few shops and dilatory streets
Raging with heat during the dinner hour---
It seemed odd
That such a small hurt should land us there.
For what reason really?
So are the years tendered, gratefully set,
The intolerable stretch made tolerable.
"We have got this far"---and know the next step,
And look about and make ready.
The room was plumped, curtains drawn,
Hushed with good appointment.
It was the right thing to do.

                                                    Under

Under morning's blameless sky,
It all became quite clear,
Repeating ourselves,
That loss is a form of celebration,
A slipping away by agreed-on stages---
In the stillness of the breakfast cove,
Before pulling the car around for cases
      and a snapshot.
So we picked up again,
Eastward, along the smooth corridor,
With scarce a turning to deflect the hum
Of what could only be joy
Insensible.
Not looking to right or left
Or back or over the hill;
While summer, what was left of it,
Calendar-hung,
Issued such days as one could not think on.

Love Song

A rose is mystery at hand,
Song and essence to command,
Till in a breath the petals fall
To silence by a garden wall.

God is mystery from afar:
Beams an intermittent star
Of wondrous beauty half found out,
Lost in plenitude or drought.

You are mystery everywhere,
In chamber or a hemisphere,
Who still the waves of helplessness
And knit the knotted hour of peace.

The Robin

The sea bird has no song
But cries the silent winds among
Where suns and constellations pass
A solitary note of wrong
    Above the heaving mass.

    My robin takes the breeze
To carol earth's conveniences;
A garden prodigal of May,
Snuggery of house and trees
    And friend to catch the lay.

    It picks the shortest flight;
No robin trial of breadth and height
Nor broach of transcendental zone,
But keeps a cottage day and night
    And wakes the summer dawn.

IV.
The Home-Place

Stopping By

The first ray of sun
    On an old faded wall
Knocks at the heart---
    Oh, let us call!
But all, all have vanished,
    Set off in the night---
No lift of latch
    In the yellow light.

The Home-Place

You know it all before you get there---
In sparsity of tree and sap,
The unmistakable leveling off,
And death's convocation in the vine's clamber.
This is where they come back,
If they do come back,
Pausing at the smokehouse door,
The tree by the watershelf,
Or broken sill where a plowpoint rusts.
In the winter storm at midnight,
They cry, poor things,
Out of the wind's dissolution
To set up again, sweet ghosts,
For an April morning
And to build the chimney back!
Not grave-ridden with a hamper of bones
But free young spirits,
Ready to work,
Waiting!
Here in the waste of cow-itch vine
Where no one comes any more,
They wait.
You feel that,
You feel that first coming up the hill.

Decoration Day

These are not the flowers she knew;
In her garden lilac grew,
Pinks, sweet William, hollyhock,
An old rose fragrant by the walk.

I bring the flowers that have no scent,
Bereft of time and element,
Forever here to bud or bloom
Plastic grief beside a tomb.

Leaving

After a good visit, when I leave home
Driving around the house with the dogs in tow
And a face hanging in the window,
I submit to an old shame.
Is it a sign, I ask myself, of weak timber---
Or only a game, on both sides self-deceiving,
Trying to hold on in a time of slippage?
And what if I did---
If I did turn round at the mailbox
And, startling at the door---
What would there be to say?
The putting away of tears forever
And facing up to love in the morning.
One glance back from the road
(One time he called me back,
Waving something over his head),
The old house, resigned already,
Settles into vexed ways.
Leaving unanswered the old question:
How far can the heart be trusted,
Leaving home alone,
When light, cascading, splinters in the pear tree
On a perfectly ordinary winter afternoon?

The Note

The message was brief enough---
    Four words to be exact---
But closed the account forever,
    No appeal to fact.

I ratified the verdict;
    All mortal things below
Bend in suppliance for an hour
    And take their turn. Although

This case would not have happened
    But some officious clown
Found a piece of paper
    And wrote the sentence down.

The Whippoorwills

Before dawn I heard the whippoorwills,
Skirting the orchard stillness, strangely near
An open window, harboring in the dark
Dark notes of joy and fear;
For days were drawing out. July nests were cold.
They stayed too long that year.

And on that day my father died.
Did those birds stay to tell
And shape an old ungarnered woe
In bright oracle?
Or was it a cry for our dear lost woods,
Where spring had done so well?

The Wanton

The dead, defeated, have no mercy!
    Through the drained hours in trivial glee,
Dropping in derelict doors a promise,
    Bantering an old delinquency.

Waiting in a window, backward talking,
    When I entered, she turned and laughed---
In whispering gowns again distracted---
    Only I could catch that drift!

No mercy, poor lost ones! Why should they,
    Out of the silent, friendless bourne
Tapping, tapping at midnight pillows
    In the mock night of love's return?

The Bluebird

When the bluebird built in our mailbox,
We tore it out, little bird!
Fluttering, with your mate looking on---
Settling again on the ruins
When we went back to the house.
Now there is no race of blue in the morning.
There are no mailboxes,
No fenceposts with knotholes
In sweet pastures by the creekside, -
Nor cows that graze so peacefully.

The Cornfield

I found the picture in a corner bay
Breathing, though a hundred years were gone,
The sweet content of a summer day
In green and gold under an English sun.
Dappled with bright flowers the cornfield shone
And rooks sailed in from a dark wood far away.

A village steeple, modest and true,
Beyond the field and wood in noon's white light
Called to the parish, strong in pith and thew,
Caroling the day at sun's height,
To think upon the coming of the night
And them beneath the cypress and the yew.

And, turning from that tiny frame,
The earth, though more than ever sweet
Racked with another May, was not the same.
Voices long silent at my feet
By billows lifted on the yellow wheat
Rose on the chastened air and called my name.

V.
Fall Morning

Fall Morning

The old year holds on too long,
An errant Gulf remembering.
Dawn upbraids the tardiness of seasons,
For not getting on with it---
While a red rose enjoins the day
And from willow oaks, flexing gold,
Blackbirds take off for the cornfields.
What business has beauty beyond its time?
East is revelation beyond the claims of clay,
Grown cold
Among mud huts and parked cars,
Where the street light still burns.

Goldenrod

Flower of waste places,
    Whose heart was set on gold,
How the year comes down to
    Indigence of weed.

No token of heaven,
    No flame, no flare of wood---
Only the dusty beacon
    Racked sod allowed.

Fido

There was a providence in how we met!
Canine nature, cold and wet,
Shook with shaggy joy and pled
To undertake my secret need.

His bruised heart was set to come.
I wanted to take him home,
Bind his wounds, give him bread,
And put my friend warm to bed;

But left him by the lonely wood.
My kind of love he understood---
And lay down for another day
His master might come down that way.

The Snake

One fine day
The yellow snake lay in the chicken house,
Its great length stretched along the crossbeam,
Waiting.
The hens, withdrawn sedately, clacked
In dim recall of night's tremendous rape.
Hung in mass
In dusty air ingesting,
Putting an edge on light.

Cedars

On this dark slope
White with the rot of an inland sea,
Pocahontas might have reigned,
Braided like a flower child,
Doing the honors of auto-da-fé.
And while the poor naked wretch,
Grapevine-noosed to a sycamore,
Danced for the dear children,
Though rather too far from center---
Those were the days!---
The Princess rallied the fire brigade.
After the London season, the children languished.
Paste and gaud brought back, worthless sham---
And the mystery of green was gone:
The cry in the vale,
Eyes that see and tell,
And tell the truth before the sun goes down!
Now there is no news, no knowledge,
No visitation of the gods
Among the cedars and oyster shells.
And nothing at all to get up to in the morning.

Historical Marker

From this valley with his squaw
Ruled King Ishtehotopah,
Happy man, the story went,
Till deputation to his tent
In royal treaty acquiesced,
And moved the levee to the west.

Today, about the King's demesne
Another tribe survey the green
In work and play, joy and strife---
All the regular rules of life---
And haven't time to stand in awe
Before the sign, or care a straw
For poor King Ishtehotopah.

Putting My Dog To Sleep

She was a good sort of dog and in the afternoon
   Napped by her master's chair,
But a trick of nature got in the way---
   It was not your fault, poor dear.

Had to be helped to the waiting car,
   Baulked at so much kind address,
But lapped at last in her gentle chain
   Submitted to tenderness.

It was the best way. (But how could she know?
   Just back from her morning run!)
Only a moment to set things right,
   No fuss for anyone.

There on the strange linoleum floor
   She fell, obedient, blind---
And was led away by soft new hands.
   Let us hope they were kind.

The Little Moth

I found a moth in the window pane
And gave it sky to fly again;
Again, recalled to a corner stir,
Tried to lift a silent blur

Of clout so small I was not sure
An ache like mine was harbored there;
But blew upon the fuzz of light,
Dissolving element in flight.

Too faint to touch to give it wing!
Hardly a breath of anything;
But off to life and joy of leaf,
And, oh, its moiety of grief.

The Fugitives

This first cold day,
Searching the depths as it was meant to do
For fugitives in dark holes, crevices,
      and under stones,
Leaves a great silence where blossoms hung
And caravans met on a blade of grass.
Summer betrayed us;
The tents are broken, the minions departed.
In this chambered hush where justice reigns---
No stay, no stay!
Only a still requiem
For all the little things
That don't live around here anymore.

The Blessing

Morning breaks in benison
    On emperor and king;
On every cock that from his hill
    Triumphantly doth sing;
On the poor wethered shepherd boy,
    The bird with pinioned wing,
And at the new day's Judgment Seat
    Each little trembling thing.

VI.
Nightshade

The Virgin

There he stands in honor's brow
Wonderfully concentrated before action.
Flesh recoils before that decimated self,
That lean abandon and winged gaze---
Reserved down here for pulpit and park bench.
We crane and grin and wait for the others
      to catch up.
Not fair when you come to think about it,
A stone saint forever poised,
Virgin among pigeons,
Meddling in the pieties of the traffic circle.
Down here we like to take our shoes off.
How can he stand it, all the year round,
Pitching in the sky that dumb stuck look?

In The Radiation Therapy
Waiting Room

They loll like voyagers, relaxed, debonaire,
    About to set off on the ocean's breadth;
No in-house slogans, no magazines here
    (All very well for the pulling of teeth),

But blather and fun, looking over our heads
    With purse-proud eyes---though circumspect,
Mindful of those without the quids
    To undertake passage with this elect.

They blink at the thought of perilous seas
    And a dark night's stake of bankrupt sail---
With this klieg light, these auspices,
    And four tight walls invulnerable.

We fall back dumb, keeping our place
    Till time for our seasoned betters to embark,
Hugging their pride with wheel-chair grace
    Up the gangway to Noah's Ark.

The Beacon

Specs new riveted
With head aslant to catch the kitchen light,
She settles down to news.
"Lightning Strikes New Home Church,"
"County Opts for Flood Control," and---
Narrowing the focus---
"Brother J. P. Wardlaw, Crossing Cane Creek
   Bottom Wednesday Night..."
All very satisfactory.
Beyond the county line
Roads take off for unfamiliar antipodes,
Past felled line trees.
Where streams flow north,
Folks rush on to unaccountable things---
Not mentioned in The Beacon,
"The Only Newspaper in the World that Cares
   Anything about Itawamba County,"
Safe in the mailbox every Thursday morning
By the time she gets her peas on.

Old Maids

They signal presence in a row
    To honor Mr. Zinn,
Bosom starched and studied,
    Musk and essence thin;

And make a play in August,
    Entreating, shrill,
Hiding in a painted prop
    Stint of chlorophyll.

The Daisy Tree

What flower is this,
Rising out of the dust like a kapok tree?
The front porch, rickety with pots and pans
A little worse for October,
Leans in proud possession.
Relict of riverwash and swamp hummock
    where crocodile sunned
Before the railroad came to rattle the
    waterbucket.
Triumphant daisy tree,
Tied up like a broom with the ravelings of
    flour sacks,
Blooming its head off!
A world of pleasure in this garden.

Vieux Carré

The drunk came down out of the dark
Waving his arms across St. Philip Street,
Where the sun stalked shadows and a halo of hair.
From the balcony
Pink roofs sloped west,
Ibises floated,
And while the city slept
Morning's first car turned in from Esplanade.
The drunk, on stage now, stilled--
Turned a tactic with sleepy face, posturing peace,
Waiting for the house.
Conspiracy on the edge of dawn!
The house waited---
And the car drew on out of the mists of lower
    Royal Street,
Shouldering night,
Pulling up legions of sense,
Throwing up barricades by the river.
The Quarter, roused,
Stretched on simian walls,
Waiting debauch of sun.

Assumption

When the cyclone came in April,
Our six guineas blew clean away!
Not a feather
As we addled our way in the bright morning
 after that visitation.
Stretched now among the Pleiades,
They crossed over at half-past twelve o'clock,
Trailing Afric sands and a blackgum far away.

Nightshade

Standing by the bathroom window at two o'clock
    Fraught with love and unofficial glee,
I vow to front the day's officious knock
    And reinvest fair night's authority.

A layabout in Cassiopeia's Chair
    Swelling in state above the deep,
Forging in gold the words that never were
    Except in derelict sleep;

Dealing in posies and the lambent fall
    Of gauzy sense surprised in bliss,
Cavorting with fact of miracle---
    An old cob out to grass.

Far down the west a peaked yellow moon
    Malingers in a starry bed:
I cry, "O Queen, assume thy sequined throne!"
    And grope along the passage back to bed.

VII.
Bright Star!

The Cedar

When frost first comes to the roadside,
The thicket stampedes in a mess of departure,
Faded and windblown,
Hurrying into nakedness.
But cedar and brown sage step out in
      dignified mien!
There in a field sloping up to woods
Where the sagegrass welcomes a flock of blackbirds---
And rabbits to burrows, no doubt, if I could see
      them---
The cedar stands guard,
Strong in the northwind, fresh-scented,
Riding out storms for little birds
Asleep under snow in its branches.
Clean and well-favored all winter long.

Bright Star!

Bright Star! Would I were steadfast as thou art,
Certain above men's musings!
As I go out to pick up the paper---
The daily wash of Humber and Nile
And a thousand dead bodies
In thoughtless shallows laid---
What terms, what trick of ransom
On a bleak shelf stranded?
In this thin air, above the stench,
The whetted sail turns home;
Riding the shoreless morn,
World without end,
At cockcrow.

The Rabbit

A blanched woods in early morning, frost-rimed
   by still water,
Throws on the heart
The innocent life of seeds and grasses
And all chaste creatures that startle from sight.
(The gross are sunk in sullen pools
Or withdrawn to dark places of fur and bone.)
When the sun strikes first on the willows,
The rabbit comes out to see man,
Naked and trembling by the roadside,
Helpless from covert, but trusting, trusting,
In wonder alike at the rare moment.

Ponderosas

Leaving the desert and date palm
In much good heat,
We set off through Joshua trees
For the sheep country---
Swath of green in wind tufts flower-studded---
And caught, rising in the blue,
Ponderosas,
Unlikely as heaven, on top of the world!
And went in where it was cool.
Great cones lay about and we picked up some
And saw where we were,
On Pisgah's height, God promising!

But that was long ago.
Back here
In stunted hills of blackjack
And low creek bottom
And in a different dispensation,
The prophecy falters.
Summer has no respite
(A narrow span receding),
No surety of mountain and no good heat.
But from these flats---
With an old chart huddled and racked by sky!---
We remember that elevation,
That trek through fire to where the trees waited.

Layover

Beggars, entrenched at the church door,
Stretched arms and teeth---
And one of them bit me as I entered.
Inside it was cool, and the world was on its knees---
On Monday afternoon!
Mr. Anglo-Saxon stood up,
Looked round about with pesos in his pocket
And said, "What's this? What's this?"
But sat down again. And caught the Virgin in
    a skylight,
In blue, with flowers.
(How did they get up there to do that?)
A black mantilla came with a sparkle
And a young man who signed thrice and fell to
    his sins.
And beggars, of course,
Circulating through the afternoon like a
    water fountain,
On knees with mean eyes,
Counting their money.
The pew sign said, "Watch your purse!"
But the Virgin kept us, from her high throne sky-lifted,
Cutting down time in the strangest way,
Exalting old cankers,
Directing the saints in their good offices
From dark corners, watching.
In church together,
That moment, that Monday afternoon at half-past two,
While a train waited to cross the mountain.
It was the best place to go.

The Swallow

In good King Alfred's day,
Light was official mystery!
Between dark and dark, chanced in a patch of sun
The life of swineherd, scribe, and king upon
      his throne---
Like the night-swallow's flight through a
      lighted room.
And I, upon this winter afternoon
Marveling at a blanched elm against the sky
And the sun still on my back,
Reintroduce beside my kitchen door
Affairs of state, on which a thousand years ago
A Witan took full note.

The Elect

How should the likes of me
That have some sorry want in everything
And to each turn a cross-grained spirit bring
    Smack such sweet liberty?

    Why should the gates make way
To issue a puny slip from death
While armies jostle to hang one breath
    On a summer day?

    And why that day so bright
While dun toilers who never shirk
Trim their passage to the waiting dark
    And leave me in the light!

    As well exalt a worm
While height and beauty in strength begot
Fall to earth by the fowler's shot---
    And it can only squirm.

    Or an ill-natured weed,
The squatter who pays no rent
But sticks the tender bud of blush and scent
    And frowns and falls to seed.

    Why the swarming bat
When music once hermited the wood?---
It is the grace and favor of God,
    The first aristocrat,
                  Who,

    Who, with purblind eye
And deaf imperious ear
And old man's knack for the rum and queer,
    Arrays His rude chivalry.

    Like spastic soldiers in a row,
We fall in to unseemly pranks,
And He looks out from His stand and winks
    On the poor ribald show.